Living in New Lanark

a brief guide to the history of housing in the village

Contents

Preface

New Lanark was a brand new industrial settlement at the end of the 18th century, and renowned as a model village under the enlightened management of Robert Owen in the early 1800s. At the end of the 20th century, it has won fame again, as the largest conservation project in Europe, and as an industrial heritage site of world significance.

The project to restore the entire village, while preserving New Lanark as a living, working community, began in 1963 with the formation of New Lanark Association Ltd, one of the earliest housing associations, and was strengthened immeasurably by the founding of New Lanark Conservation Trust in 1974.

This booklet aims to give a brief history of the New Lanark housing. All proceeds from its sale help the New Lanark Conservation Trust in its continuing work of restoring and revitalising the historic village.

Chapter 1: Workers' Housing

When David Dale chose a riverside site in rural Scotland for his new cotton-mills in 1785, commuting to work was an unknown concept, and factory-working hardly any more familiar. Housing had to be provided, partly because people expected to live close to their place of work, and partly to encourage them to take up employment in the mills – a prospect which was not immediately attractive to a rural pre-industrial population.

According to the *Old Statistical Account*[1] for Lanarkshire, written in 1795, a workforce of 90 stonemasons, joiners and labourers had been employed at New Lanark for the past 10 years in erecting buildings, both mills and dwelling-houses. The site was a difficult one, in terms of the very limited amount of flat land available for building along the river-bank.

Tall tenements were the solution to the problem of scarce building land, and indeed this style was a long established tradition in Edinburgh and Glasgow. It was unusual, however, in a rural area, and the imposing stone-built tenements with their rows and rows of small-paned windows are unexpectedly beautiful examples of industrial architecture in the countryside.

The masons who undertook the work (and it is believed that a master-mason rather than an architect supervised the enterprise) were faced with the additional problem of building on the rising land at the foot of the valley, and all the tenements have at least one floor which is a semi-basement, with windows to the south side only.

The stonework is an enduringly attractive feature of New Lanark. The houses were strongly built in the style known as "random rubble". The locally quarried sandstone was not cut into regular blocks; instead, the natural shapes of the stones were used at random. Around the doors, windows and corners, a light-coloured dressed sandstone was used.

[1] Sir J. Sinclair (ed.) *The Old Statistical Account of Scotland, Vol XV.* A survey of Scotland carried out in the late 18th century, parish by parish.

It is known that some thatch was used at first, but this was soon replaced by slate roofing, which, as Dale remarked in a letter to a friend in 1792, was *"best and cheapest in the end, and not so subject to accidents as thatch roofs."*

It is not known exactly when or in what order the original houses were built, though it is likely that they were the dwellings closest to Mill No. One, i.e. Double Row, Wee Row, Long Row, and Braxfield Row. The earliest known prints of the village, by Robert Scott, date from the 1790s and show these rows fully in place, as is Caithness Row at the eastern end of the village. The latter was built in response to a pledge by Dale to provide houses for 200 Highlanders, and this work was finished in the summer of 1793. Like the other villagers, they rented their homes from the owner of the mills.

In the early days of the village's existence, the living conditions were extremely crowded by modern standards (though perfectly normal at the time). By 1796, the population of the village had reached 1,519, including almost 400 young apprentices, mostly orphans and paupers from Glasgow and Edinburgh. Only one room was allocated to each family, and the child apprentices slept three to a bed.

New Lanark Mills by Robert Scott

Chapter 2: Owners' and Managers' Housing

New Lanark c. 1818 from an original by John Winning

In addition to the rows of tenements designed to accommodate the millworkers, two detached houses were built in the centre of the village. One of these, a pleasantly proportioned house with wings to east and west, was used by David Dale on his visits to New Lanark. His main residence was a substantial town-house designed by Robert Adam in Charlotte Street in Glasgow (sadly demolished in the 1950s) but his five daughters were conveyed to the "cottage" at New Lanark to benefit from the country air during the summer months.

Next door was another house, which may originally have been occupied by James Dale, a half-brother of David Dale, who managed the New Lanark mills for him. Subsequently, both houses were used by the mill managers, the most famous of whom was Robert Owen, Dale's son-in-law. He married David Dale's eldest daughter Anne Caroline in 1799, and the couple took up residence in the village when Owen became the managing partner of the company on the 1st January 1800.

Though modest by comparison with Dale's imposing house in Charlotte Street, where Robert and Caroline were married, the Managers' houses at New Lanark were considerably more spacious than the tenement rooms allocated to the workforce, and moreover were equipped with internal water supply and sanitation at a much earlier stage than the workers' homes. Internally, they have undergone many changes since they were first built at the end of the 18th century; indeed by the 1880s, one of them had been divided into two self-contained flats.

The Valuation Survey of 1903, carried out for the Gourock Ropework Company, described the properties in the following terms:

"Rosedale" – villa occupied as Manager's house, two storeys in height with attic floor in addition, containing five rooms and kitchen with bathroom on ground floor, four bedrooms on first floor and two bedrooms in attic.

"Village House" – two storey building with basement and attic floors in addition, occupied as two separate dwelling-houses, the ground floor house having three rooms and kitchen with bathroom and wash-house in basement, and the upper floor house having five rooms and kitchen with bathroom . . . . the manager's house internally has been practically rebuilt and a new bathroom put in, and Village House has also been thoroughly overhauled internally and baths and water closets provided."

Known today as David Dale's House and Robert Owen's House, these are the only detached properties in the village. During restoration, in common with the other village housing, original features have been retained or reinstated wherever this is compatible with modern building regulations. They remain in the ownership of the New Lanark Association. David Dale's House is rented out, and Robert Owen's House is open to the public.

"Robert Owen's House" after restoration.

6

Chapter 3:
Robert Owen's Management 1800-1825

In 1800, Robert Owen, the son-in-law of David Dale, became the managing partner of the New Lanark cotton-mills. He saw this as the opportunity to put into practice a social experiment which would demonstrate to the world in general that the fast-developing industrial society need not mean misery for the workforce which supported it.

Among the many social and educational reforms which Owen introduced, improvements to the housing conditions of his workers were particularly important for the health and morale of the villagers. Attributing at least some of the problems to overcrowding, Owen set about increasing the provision of housing, to allow the allocation of an extra room to families. In the words of "One formerly a teacher at New Lanark" in a pamphlet published in 1839, Owen "collected masons and joiners from the surrounding country, and set eagerly to work."[2]

The block known as "Nursery Buildings" was originally constructed as an apprentice house, and was part of Owen's plan to phase out the practice of having child workers boarding in the mill area. These pauper apprentices, who received board and lodgings in lieu of wages, formed a substantial part of Dale's workforce, numbering 396 in 1790, and rising to between 400 and 500, aged from 5 to 10 years, when Owen took over in 1800. They were housed in the upper part of Mill Four, and though they were well treated by Dale, this system did not find favour with Owen who was opposed in principle to the use of child labour.

A clue to Nursery Buildings' original function lies in its single (controllable) entrance and turnpike stair, as opposed to the normal tenement pattern of separate entrance closes and internal stairs that is common to the other village housing. As the apprentices grew up, and Owen ceased to employ young children in the mills, Nursery Buildings became available to increase the amount of accommodation that was available for families.

---

[2] *Robert Owen at New Lanark, with a variety of interesting anecdotes, by one formerly a teacher at New Lanark* Manchester, 1839.

Robert Owen was not impressed by the domestic circumstances which prevailed at the time of his arrival as manager, a state of affairs which may be deduced from some of the new regulations which he found necessary to draw up – we paraphase:

♦ that each house shall be washed at least once every week and whitewashed annually

♦ that every public stair be kept clean by its users in weekly rotation

♦ neither water, ashes, nor any other matter shall be thrown over the window, or be put near the door, but be carried to the nearest place appointed

♦ neither cattle, swine, poultry nor dogs be kept in the houses.

(Here we should remember that a fair proportion of the inhabitants at this point came originally from the Highlands where it was a perfectly normal practice for animals and people to live under the same roof).

While Owen could, and did, arrange for the cleaning of the streets and removal of sewage on a daily basis, the care of the interiors was rather more difficult. He arranged for lectures on cleanliness and hygiene, but in order to ensure that his regulations were being carried out, he asked the villagers to appoint from among themselves a committee who would inspect the houses weekly, a suggestion which met at first with rage and opposition, especially from the women. However, the "Bug-hunters", as they were promptly nicknamed, persevered, with Owen's support, and apparently with some success, as visitors to the village were soon to comment favourably on the clean and healthy appearance of the villagers. In the words of Edward Baines, the inhabitants of New Lanark were in general "clean, healthy and sober . . . . well clad, well fed and their dwellings were inviting".[3]

[3] Edward Baines MP, who visited New Lanark in 1819, at the request of the Poor Law Commissioners of Leeds, to report on Owen's system. *Mr Owen's Establishment at New Lanark, A Failure!!* Leeds, 1838.

No internal sanitation was available in the millworkers' houses at this time, but Owen's "Institute for the Formation of Character" – effectively a community education centre – was fitted up with "elegant and usefully constructed bathing machines, for the purpose of promoting health and cleanliness of the children"[4] and "conveniencies calculated to give the children such habits as will enable the master of police to keep the village in a decent, clean state".[5]

As well as improving housing conditions, Owen encouraged gardening and healthy exercise. "There has long been granted to each householder at New Lanark a portion of garden-ground to cultivate, but in order to increase the supply of vegetable food, a new public garden has been laid out by the company, which is to extend to seven or eight acres. It is surrounded by a belt of planting, and a spacious walk for the recreation of the work-people".[6]

[4] *Robert Owen at New Lanark, with a variety of interesting anecdotes by one formerly a teacher at New Lanark* Manchester, 1839.

[5] Robert Owen, *A Statement Regarding the New Lanark Establishment* Edinburgh, 1812.

[6] Dr Henry McNab, *The New Views of Mr Owen impartially examined* London, 1819.

Chapter 4: A Millworkers' Home around 1800

Although the actual buildings which housed the millworkers can still be seen today, we have no pictorial record of the interiors of the early 19th century. A combination of travellers' accounts and substantial remaining physical evidence in the form of, for example, some original fireplaces and set-in beds, has allowed us to reconstruct a room which gives an impression of living conditions in the early 19th century. This can be seen in the Millworkers' House exhibition on the ground floor of New Buildings. A typical room plan is given on page 16.

Sleeping arrangements

A typical tenement room had two "set-in" beds on the wall opposite the fireplace. These consisted of a sturdy wooden framework, with slats or "bed-boards" on which to lay a simple mattress. This was a bag made of ticking and stuffed with chaff or straw which could be obtained from the local farms, a practice which persisted well into the 20th century. The bed-boards were taken out and scrubbed as part of the spring-cleaning operations, and the straw was changed from time to time, "in general once a month" according to David Dale's account of his apprentice children's living conditions. As a contributor to the New Lanark Oral History Archive recalled ruefully, the first few nights with new straw could be uncomfortable till the "thistles and jaggy bits" got pressed down!

Sleeping space was at a premium when the same village housing which can now accommodate about 225 people had the best part of two and a half thousand crammed into it. The solution to this problem was the "hurlie bed". This was a simple cot-like bed on wheels, made entirely of wood, which was stored underneath the set-in bed during the day, and brought out at night to provide a resting place for assorted members of the family, or even a lodger! Take the Gallacher family recorded by the 1861 Census living in New Buildings in just one room with a window: there were a man, his wife, four children, a sister-in-law and two lodgers! Another contributor to the Oral History Archive recalled that as a boy in the 1920s he shared a bed with three of his brothers – two at the top and two at the bottom.

Curtains could be drawn across the front of the "set-in" bed to provide a modicum of privacy and to keep out draughts. Sheets were made of woven linen or cotton, and blankets were of wool. These were precious possessions, and when they wore a bit thin, were cut in half and turned "sides to middle" to prolong their life.

An original wooden "hurlie bed"

"A coal fire provided warmth and cheer . . . ."

Heating and Lighting

A coal fire provided warmth and cheer, and, as anyone who has dealt with an open fire will know, plenty of dust, soot and hard work too. The original fireplaces, of which several have survived, were made of cast iron, with a swinging arm or "swee" from which to hang a cooking pot or kettle over the smouldering coals. There was no oven, but pots could be simmered on the hobs to either side, or heated on metal trivets attached to the fire bars. It was a matter of pride to keep the fireplace well-swept and black-leaded.

A simple wooden mantelpiece was placed above the fire. Tallow candles would cast flickering shadows around the room when the wooden shutters were closed for the night, while oil lamps provided a steadier flame. Whale-oil was commonly used before advancing technology provided gas-lighting and paraffin lamps. It is not known exactly when the gas-making plant at New Lanark was built, but it was certainly there by 1851. Gas-lights were then installed in the village houses and streets.

Sanitation

The lack of an internal water supply was perhaps the greatest problem of all in the 19th century workers' dwelling. Every drop of water for washing and cooking had to be carried into the house in wooden buckets from the wells out in the village, and the slops trailed back out again. Nothing more convenient than a chamber-pot was available to the villagers within their own walls, although earth closets were dotted around the village, and as we saw on page 8, the places designated as middens were cleared daily. The curved recesses in the stone walls opposite Braxfield Row and Caithness Row mark the locations of the 19th century middens.

The village never reached the state of unspeakable filth and disease which was reported by 19th century travellers to Glasgow and Edinburgh, where some of the streets in the crowded urban slums were little better than open sewers. The rural location of the mill village was one saving factor, while the river Clyde flowing past provided a means of washing; one of John Winning's water-colour views of the village, dating from around 1818, shows women with wooden wash-tubs on the river-bank below Double Row.

".... women with wooden wash-tubs on the river-bank ...."

12

".... a comfortable habitation with good furniture ...."

Furnishings

Dr Henry McNab[7] visiting New Lanark in 1819 described the home of a millworker he encountered as a comfortable habitation with good furniture. This was likely to have consisted of, in addition to the beds described above, a plain wooden dresser, some simple stools and chairs, a table and a "kist" or chest. Comfort would not extend to the carpets, curtains and upholstered furniture of the fashionable Georgian dwellings inhabited by the likes of Dr McNab and his employer the Duke of Kent. Nevertheless, living conditions in New Lanark compared favourably to those of the grim slum dwellings which were all too prevalent in the great industrial cities of the 19th century. As late as 1886, a third of families in Glasgow lived in just one room.

[7] Henry McNab, *The New Views of Mr. Owen Impartially Examined* London, 1819

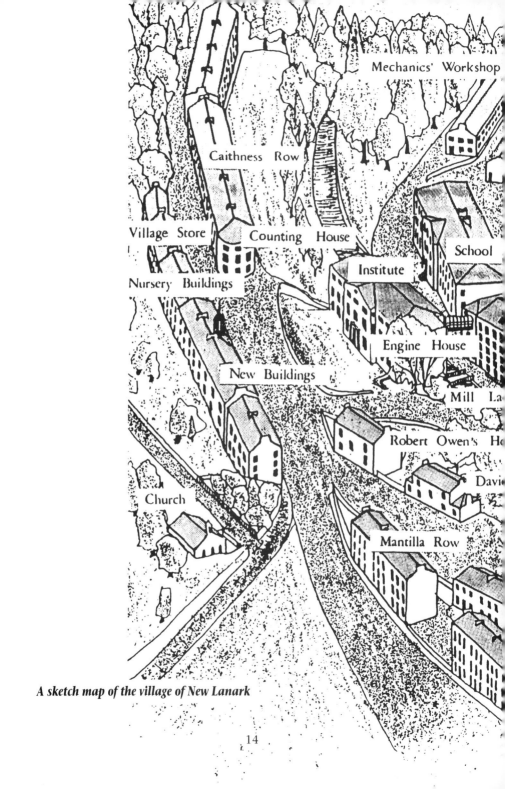

Mechanics' Workshop

Caithness Row

Village Store

Counting House

School

Nursery Buildings

Institute

Engine House

New Buildings

Mill La

Robert Owen's H

Davi

Church

Mantilla Row

A sketch map of the village of New Lanark

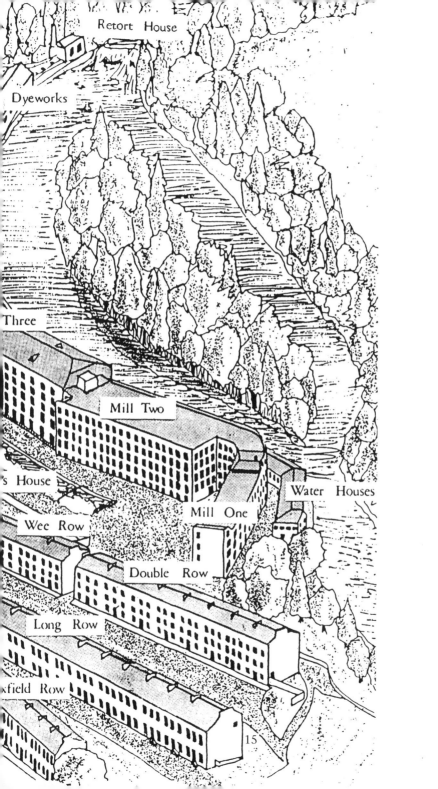

Retort House

Dyeworks

Three

Mill Two

's House

Water Houses

Wee Row

Mill One

Double Row

Long Row

xfield Row

15

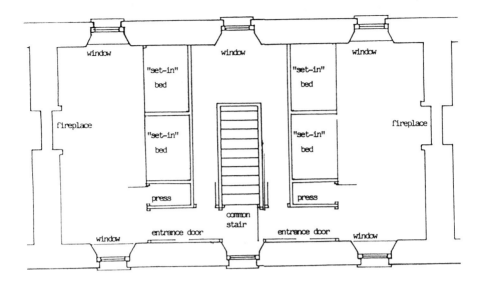

A typical 19th century room plan in a New Lanark tenement

Two separate families would have lived in the two "single-end" houses which are shown. This could mean a total of as many as 18 or 20 people.

Chapter 5: From the 1880s to the 1920s

In 1881, the mills, which had passed into the ownership of Robert Owen's friends the Walkers after 1825, were taken over by a new partnership. Under the management of Henry Birkmyre, the village housing underwent some modernisation, and when in 1903 the mills became part of the Birkmyre family firm, the Gourock Ropework Company, a Valuation Survey was carried out which provides much useful information about the village buildings.

Heating and Lighting

Homes were still heated by means of a coal fire, though, as an old villager put it, you had to crowd round about the fire on a cold winter's night to get your share; there was linoleum on the floor, but it didn't help much. Cooking was still largely done on the fire, though as time went on, oven grates became popular, with a baking oven at one side of the fire. A slight increase in rent was charged if one of these was fitted.

In 1898, the gas-lighting was superseded by hydro-electricity, when a dynamo was attached to one of the new water-turbines that replaced the old water-wheels. At the forefront of technology in the late 19th century, as it had been 100 years before when the mills were founded, New Lanark had one of the first public electrical lighting systems. Every room had its glass bulb emitting a steady, if not very powerful light. There was a snag: the supply, though free, was controlled by the mill engineers and was switched off at 10pm, 11pm on Saturdays, except in the case of a nocturnal domestic emergency, such as childbirth, when you could ask the nightwatchman to switch it on again. Paraffin lamps and primus stoves were still in common use, and the lower room in the Counting House across from the Village Store was the Paraffin Store.

The improvements to living conditions which had taken place by the end of the 19th century were partly the result of improvements in technology, and partly of a gradual decrease in the population of the village. The population of New Lanark, estimated at 2,500 in 1818, had dropped to just 795 by 1901. The majority of households now had two rooms, while 56 of the basement rooms, no longer required for living accommodation, were converted into communal wash-houses and cellarage.

Sanitation

The dry closets were replaced by flushing water closets around 1900, but these were still outside the houses, except in the case of the Managers' Houses and the Doctor's House and Surgery which was located in New Buildings. The 1903 Valuation Survey states that "A complete drainage system has recently been introduced, with septic tank for the purification of the sewage before discharging into the Clyde, and outside conveniences for the tenants have also been erected. An ample domestic supply of spring water from the adjoining hillside has also been introduced, with new stand wells in front of the houses, and internal supplies to the Managers' houses."

"The Wash-house" – Millworkers' House Exhibition

Despite the provision of the wash-houses, the weekly wash was still a heavy task. Water had to be carried from stand-wells outside, to fill the tubs and boilers, and a coal fire had to be kindled underneath to heat it. To the women who struggled with mangles, wringers, dollies, wash-boards, tongs, tubs and the dead weight of dripping laundry, the automatic washing machine in common use today would have seemed little short of miraculous.

Chapter 6: From the 1930s – 1950s

In 1933, the houses were fitted with a "jawbox" or kitchen sink and a supply of cold water was piped round the village to replace the old stand-wells. Internal sanitation was long in coming, and did not reach the workers' homes until 1933. Indoor lavatories, shared in most cases by neighbouring households, were installed on the landings and were known as the "stairheid cludgies".

1930s kitchen sink

The old-fashioned "set-in" beds remained in most homes until the 1940s, at least in one room. As living space increased, and the "room and kitchen" arrangement became common, the beds were often removed from the kitchen. By the 1960s, when the programme of housing restoration began, most of the old beds had been taken out, in some cases to make way for an inside lavatory.

Electrical appliances became increasingly common, and the system provided by the mill suffered constantly from blown fuses as enterprising villagers attempted to connect up electric irons, radios and the like. Finally in 1955, the mills gave up the unequal struggle, and the houses were connected to the national grid. The Company continued to generate hydro-electricity, which was now cabled round the mills to drive the machinery.

Changes there had certainly been, but some things remained the same. The houses were still owned by the Company, and families living in them had to have at least one member working in the mills. Permission for any moves within the village, or for the allocation of a house to a young couple planning to marry, had to be sought from the Manager. Rents were low, but so were the wages. To its credit, the Gourock Ropework Company was conscious that it had inherited an important piece of history, and its efforts to maintain the housing, long before the buildings were officially designated as being of historic significance, were rewarded in 1957 with a commendation from the Saltire Society.

Chapter 7: Mill Closure and Crisis

After 1945, a series of new building regulations came into force which gradually rendered most of the New Lanark housing stock sub-standard. The Gourock Ropework Company, struggling to adapt its traditional cotton-manufacturing capacity to the introduction of the highly popular man-made fibres, felt that it could not afford the substantial investment required to upgrade the old tenements. The housing was offered at a nominal price to the local authority, but was refused because so much restoration was needed.

In 1963, with the co-operation of the Company, a housing association known as New Lanark Association was formed, and ownership of all the tenement housing was transferred to this new body for £250. An initial programme of restoration was drawn up, and work began on Caithness Row and Nursery Buildings to create 25 tenancies within the original buildings.

In March 1968, the Gourock Ropework Company announced the closure of its New Lanark Mills, precipitating a rapid decline in the village population, a widespread loss of faith in the future of New Lanark, and the housing restoration, already facing financial problems, ground to a halt. In common with the other mill buildings, the old tenements presented a sad and deteriorating picture.

In the face of a very real threat that most of the village would be demolished, a Working Party was established to consider the future of New Lanark. Its report, published in 1973, recommended the formation of the New Lanark Conservation Trust which was duly formed the following year, to assist the housing association and promote the restoration of the entire village.

The village was designated an "Outstanding Conservation Area" and all the buildings are now Listed in Category "A", Scotland's highest in terms of historic and architectural significance.

The restoration work was given an enormous boost when New Lanark Association undertook the running of a Community Programme under the auspices of the Manpower Services Commission, a government job creation scheme designed to alleviate the high unemployment of the 1980s.

Chapter 8: Towards Restoration

Progress was painstakingly slow, but steady, and as comfortable new tenancies were created within the old sandstone tenements, with central heating, modern kitchens and bathrooms, the population statistics started to rise again, though they can never again climb much beyond 300. "New Buildings" which according to the 1841 Census housed 207 individuals in 34 separate households, now accommodates around 30 people in 16 comfortable housing association flats.

Great care was taken to preserve the historic appearance of the village, and no telephone wires, television aerials or other accessories of modern living are to be seen. Cables were concealed, and a single television aerial does duty for the entire village, with the signal cabled down from the hillside above. Priority for the allocation of these new homes was given to the families who were still living in the mill village that they regarded as home, and even in the 1990s, New Lanark had a core population of long-established village residents.

In parallel with the housing association programme, an "owner-restorer" scheme was pioneered. The restored shells of tenements in Braxfield Row and part of Long Row were sold to buyers who were then responsible for the remaining restoration work. By 1995, there were 45 tenancies and 20 owner-occupied houses in New Lanark. Not surprisingly, there is always a waiting-list for the tenancies, and the owner-occupied houses come on the market infrequently.

Restored housing at Braxfield Row

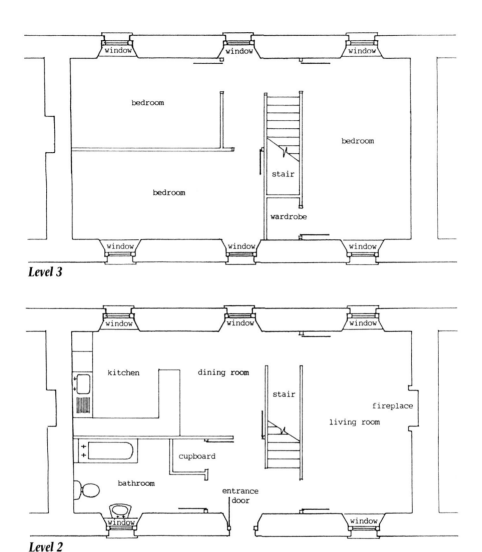

Level 3

Level 2

Level 1: general storage and cellarage

A typical plan of a restored house in Long Row.

Compare this with the plan on page 16. On average 4 people live in the space shown above.

"Wee Row", in a variation to the established pattern of housing restoration, was refurbished as a joint project between the New Lanark Conservation Trust and the Scottish Youth Hostels Association. It opened as a modern 62-bed hostel in the summer of 1994, to offer accommodation to some of the many thousands of visitors who now come to New Lanark from all over the world. Wee Row is a good example of the substantial expenditure involved in restoring these historic buildings, having cost about £1 million.

The Wee Row Youth Hostel opened in 1994

By 1995, two tenement blocks remained to be restored: Double Row, of which the exterior had been completed as part of the Manpower Services Commission Community Programme, and Mantilla Row (recorded as Mount Hooly Row in the early Census Records). This last had in fact to be completely dismantled during the 1980s in order to reconstruct the foundations before restoration was possible.

At the far end of Double Row is a single tenement stair which will not be gutted and modernised. Here remain the least altered rooms, some still with their set-in beds, inhabited until the late 1970s by an old lady who preferred not to change them. This stair will be restored as a testament to the living conditions of an earlier age. However, its original wooden stairs and restricted access preclude its use as part of the Visitor Centre. Instead, a Millworkers' House exhibition has been created in the ground floor of New Buildings, so that visitors can see reconstructed homes of the 1820s and 1930s, a wash-house and even a "stairheid cludgie". Wherever possible, original artefacts saved during the restoration work have been used. The 1820s room is beyond living memory, but in the 1930s home, it is fascinating to watch the mixture of nostalgia and relief which characterises the reactions of visitors who recognise all too easily the black-leading brush lying at the hearth, and the sink at the window with its one cold tap – nostalgia for a lost way of life, relief that modern technology has done away with many back-breaking chores.

An original "stairheid cludgie"

Chapter 9:
Preservation of a Living Community

In 1987, New Lanark was awarded the Europa Nostra Silver Medal of Honour for the outstanding conservation work undertaken to restore the buildings around the village square and preserve a living community within the historic mill village. This is Europe's highest award for conservation. The village does indeed still live, and the New Lanark Village Group, to which about 90% of the inhabitants belong, acts both as a residents' association and a social group, organising activities throughout the year for young and old.

Many observers have commented on the friendliness of the village. Asked about this community spirit, the last Works Manager of the New Lanark cotton-mills, interviewed in 1984 for the New Lanark Oral History Archive replied:

"That was threaded through it all. And it must have been something inherited, I would think. Because the village folk especially, and they were very much in the majority when I went there at first, their attitude was to their work and to their neighbour, you know they did co-operate very well indeed. And I think others coming in from elsewhere found this when they came in, and just became part of it. They had a strong liking towards each other, you know, within a department. They worked together and co-operated with each other. And I think that was something that must have been inherited by the villagers themselves."

The pen and ink drawings in this book are taken from originals by Malcolm Grieve in the Millworkers' House Exhibition.

For more information about New Lanark please contact:

New Lanark Conservation Trust
New Lanark Mills
Lanark
ML11 9DB

Tel: (01555) 661345
Fax: (01555) 665738

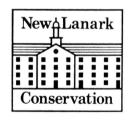

© New Lanark Conservation Trust 1995

ISBN 0 9522531 1 9